FLORIDA

Treasures

A Reading/Language Arts Program

Program Authors

Dr. Donald R. Bear
University of Nevada, Reno
Reno, Nevada

Dr. Jan E. Hasbrouck
Educational Consultant - J.H. Consulting
Seattle, Washington

Dr. Janice A. Dole
University of Utah
Salt Lake City, Utah

Dr. Scott G. Paris
University of Michigan
Ann Arbor, Michigan

Dr. Douglas Fisher
San Diego State University
San Diego, California

Dr. Timothy Shanahan
University of Illinois at Chicago
Chicago, Illinois

Dr. Vicki Gibson
Longmire Learning Center, Inc.
College Station, Texas

Dr. Josefina V. Tinajero
University of Texas at El Paso
El Paso, Texas

Dr. Jana Echevarria
California State University, Long Beach
Long Beach, California

Macmillan/McGraw-Hill

Unit 1

All About Us

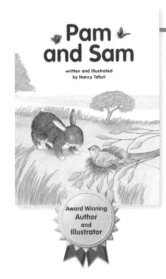

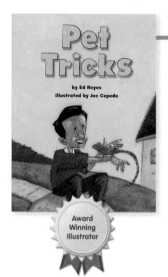

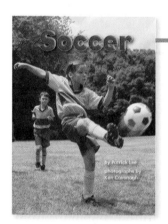

We Are Special

Talk About It

What do you like to do? What makes you special?

LOG ON Find out more about being yourself at **www.macmillanmh.com**

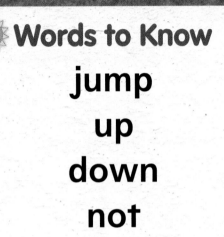

Words to Know

jump
up
down
not

P<u>a</u>t
c<u>a</u>n

Read to Find Out

Will Pat jump?

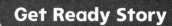

Can Pat Jump?

by Ann Carr

illustrated by
Bernard Adnet

Jump up.

Jump **down**.

Pat can **not** jump.

Look! Pat can jump!

Comprehension

Genre

A Fantasy is a made-up story that could not really happen.

Story Structure

Plot

As you read, use your **Character Chart**.

Pam Can	Sam Can
can Jump	FlY

Read to Find Out

What makes Pam and Sam special?

Pam and Sam

**written and illustrated
by Nancy Tafuri**

Pam and Sam like to play.

Pam ran **up**.

Sam ran up.

Pam and Sam ran **down**.

Pam can **jump**.

Sam can **not** jump.

Sam can not go with Pam.

Look at Sam!

Sam can fly.

Go, Pam! Go, Sam!

Say Hello to Nancy Tafuri

Nancy Tafuri says, "I live in the country and love telling stories about animals. I especially like to tell stories about good friends like Pam and Sam. I have fun drawing pictures to go with my stories."

Other books
by Nancy Tafuri

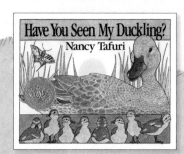

LOG ON Find out more about Nancy Tafuri at **www.macmillanmh.com**

FCAT Author's Purpose

Nancy Tafuri wanted to tell a story about friends. Draw a picture of your friend. Write your friend's name.

FCAT Comprehension Check

Retell the Story

Use the Retelling Cards to retell the story in order.

Retelling Cards

Think and Compare

Pam Can	Sam Can

1. What can Pam do? What can Sam do?

2. How are Sam and Pam like animals you have seen?

3. How do you know Pam and Sam are good friends?

4. How is Sam like Pat in "Can Pat Jump?"

27

Our Best Days

Social Studies

Genre
Nonfiction tells about real people and things.

FCAT Text Feature
Photographs give more information about the text.

Content Words
neighbor
family
friends

LOG ON Find out more about what kids like at **www.macmillanmh.com**

What day is the best day?

I like Monday.
I ride my horse.

I like Tuesday.
My **neighbor** and I play.

I like Wednesday.
My **family** has pizza.

I like Thursday.
I help my mom plant.

My **friends** and I like Friday.
What is your best day?

Connect and Compare
What might Pam and Sam do on their best day?

Write What You Like to Do

Jen wrote a sentence about painting.

I like to paint.

Your Turn

We can do many things.

What can you do?

Write about something you can do.

Writer's Checklist

☑ Did I tell what I like to do?

☑ Does my sentence tell a complete thought?

☑ Does my sentence begin with a capital letter?

Ready, Set, Move!

Talk About It

How do you like to move? What can you do?

LOG ON Find out more about movement at
www.macmillanmh.com

Words to Know

over

it

yes

too

Mac

can

Read to Find Out

What will the pigs do?

Yes, I Can!

by Alice Tu
illustrated by Diane Greenseid

Can you jump **over it**, Mac?

Yes, I can.

I can, **too**.

We can not!

Comprehension

Genre

In a **Rhyming Story**, some words end with the same sound.

Story Structure

Retell Events in Order

As you read, use your **Retelling Chart**.

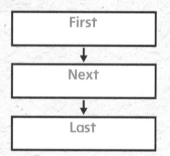

First

↓

Next

↓

Last

Read to Find Out

What will the girl and boy do together?

44

I Can! Can You?

by Cathy Roper

illustrated by Lorinda Bryan Cauley

Award
Winning
Illustrator

Can you do what I can do?

Yes! I can do **it, too.**

Can you jump **over** a mat?

Can you jump over a hat?

Can you tag a tree?

Can you tag me?

Can you tap, tap, tap?

I can nap, nap, nap.

Can you do what I can do?

Yes! I can do it, too!

Lorinda Bryan Cauley Can, Too!

Lorinda Bryan Cauley says, "I enjoy drawing children jumping, running, and playing. I always try to make each child look different from the others."

Other books by Lorinda Bryan Cauley

LOG ON Find out more about Lorinda Bryan Cauley at **www.macmillanmh.com**

Clap Your Hands
Lorinda Bryan Cauley

What Do You Know!
Lorinda Bryan Cauley

FCAT Illustrator's Purpose

Lorinda Bryan Cauley wanted to draw children playing. Draw something you do outside. Label the picture.

FCAT Comprehension Check

Retell the Story

Use the Retelling Cards to retell the story in order.

Retelling Cards

Think and Compare

1. What do the children do first? Next? Last?

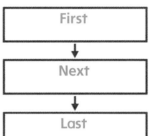

First
↓
Next
↓
Last

2. What can the children do that you can do, too?

3. What other fun outdoor things can children do together?

4. How is this story like "Yes, I Can!"?

Run! Jump! Swim!

Science

Genre
Nonfiction gives information about a topic.

Text Feature
A Label gives information about a picture.

Content Words
helps
move
push

LOG ON Find out more about how animals move at www.macmillanmh.com

What **helps** animals **move**?

tail

This dolphin can jump high.
Its strong tail helps it jump.

flippers

tail

This manatee swims slowly. Its tail and flippers help it move through the water.

tail

fins

fins

This shark can swim fast.
Its strong tail and fins **push** it
through the water.

long legs

This panther can run fast.
Its long legs help it run fast.

Kids can run, jump, and swim, too.
What helps kids move?

Connect and Compare
How could animals play with the kids
in *I Can! Can You*?

Writing

Word Order

The words in a sentence are in an order that makes sense.

Write What You Can Do

Tom wrote a sentence about skating.

I can skate.

Your Turn

Look around the room.
Think about something you can do.
Write about it.

Writer's Checklist

☑ Did I tell what I can do?

☑ Does the order of the words make sense?

☑ Does my sentence end with a special mark?

Talk About It

How have you
changed since
you were little?

 Find out more about
growing up at
www.macmillanmh.com

Growing Up

I Am a Big Kid

I am a big kid. What can I do?
I can **run**. I can **ride**.

What can I **be**?
I can be me.

How You Grew

Comprehension

Genre

A Nonfiction Article gives information about a topic.

Text Structure

FCAT Retell Events in Order

Look for things babies can do. Look for things kids can do as they get older.

How do kids change as they get older?

70

Once you were little.

You learned to talk. You could say "mama" and "puppy."

You could sit.
You could dig.

You could eat at the table.
You could sing a song.

You learned to **run** and **ride**.
You could go fast.

How big are you now?
How big will you **be**?

FCAT Comprehension Check

Tell What You Learned

Describe what kids learn to do as they get bigger.

Think and Compare

1. What can kids learn to do as they grow older?

2. Name some things you learned before you started school.

3. Name two things babies learn that are not in the story.

4. How are the kids in "I Am a Big Kid" different from the kids in "How You Grew"?

READ TOGETHER

Birds Get Big

First, a mother bird lays eggs.

Baby birds grow inside.

Then they hatch.

The mother feeds them.

The babies grow big.

Then they fly away.

Go On ▶

Directions: Answer the questions.

1. What happens first?

○   ○   ○

2. What happens after the birds hatch?

○ The birds lay eggs.

◉ The mother feeds them.

○ The birds make a nest.

Tip
Look for
key words.

3. What happens when the babies are big?

○   ○   ○

Write About Kids

First Carly drew a picture.
Then she wrote a sentence.

Big kids can ride.

FCAT Your Writing Prompt

Big kids can do many things.

Now that you are bigger, what can you do?

Write a sentence about it.

Writer's Checklist

☑ Does my sentence tell an idea?

☑ Does my sentence begin with a capital letter?

☑ Does my sentence end with a period?

Pets

Talk About It

What pets do you know? What are they like?

LOG ON Find out more about pets at **www.macmillanmh.com**

☀ Words to Know

come

that

on

good

——————

Brad

grab

Read to Find Out

Will Brad come down?

Come Down, Brad!

by Henry Chan

illustrated by Amanda Haley

Come down, Brad!

Do not grab **that!**

Jump **on** me.

What a **good** cat you are!

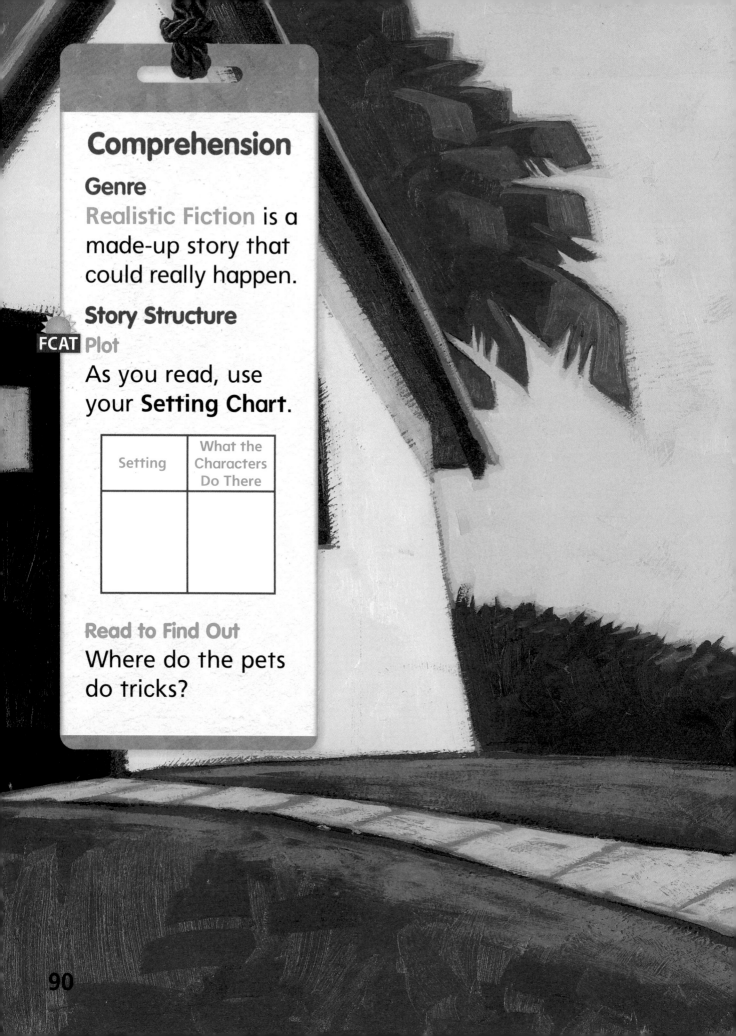

Comprehension

Genre
Realistic Fiction is a made-up story that could really happen.

Story Structure

FCAT Plot

As you read, use your **Setting Chart**.

Setting	What the Characters Do There

Read to Find Out
Where do the pets do tricks?

Pet Tricks

by Ed Reyes
illustrated by Joe Cepeda

Award
Winning
Illustrator

Come see the pets!

Come see the pet tricks.

Frizz has a **good** trick.

Frizz can jump over a bat.

Ham has a good trick.

Ham can run **on** the track.

Zig has a good trick.

Zig can grab the rope.

Can Kit do a trick?

Kit can not jump over a bat.

Kit will not grab **that** rope.

Kit can kiss!
That is a good trick.

Meet Joe Cepeda's Pets

Joe Cepeda says, "My family likes pets. My son has an iguana, a dog, and a frog. Gizzy, his iguana, goes for walks on a leash! We haven't been able to teach our dog any tricks. I think drawing animals is just like drawing people. They're just fuzzier!"

Other books by Joe Cepeda

LOG ON Find out more about Joe Cepeda at **www.macmillanmh.com**

FCAT Illustrator's Purpose

Joe Cepeda wanted to draw friendly pets. Draw a pet you like and label it.

FCAT Comprehension Check

Retell the Story

Use the Retelling Cards to retell the story in order.

Retelling Cards

Think and Compare

Setting	What the Characters Do There

1. Where does the story take place?

2. How are the animals in the story like pets you know?

3. What tricks have you seen other pets do?

4. What tricks might Brad from "Come Down, Brad!" do in a pet show?

What Pets Need

Science

Genre
Nonfiction gives information about a topic.

FCAT **Text Feature**
A List is a series of things written in order.

Content Words
need
living things
care

 Find out more about pets at **www.macmillanmh.com**

What do pets **need**?

106

Like all **living things**, pets need food. Some pets eat seeds or plants.

Some pets eat meat or fish.
All pets need fresh water.

Caring for My Rabbit

- Give it food.

- Give it water.

- Change the bedding.

- Brush the fur.

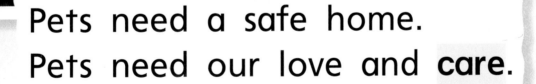

Pets need a safe home.
Pets need our love and **care**.

Connect and Compare
Which pet in *Pet Tricks* would you like?
How would you care for it?

Writing

Exclamation

An **exclamation** is a sentence that shows strong feeling.

Write About a Pet

Robert wrote about a dog.

Boo is really smart!

Your Turn

Some pets are very special.
Think about a pet you know.
Write to tell why this pet
is special.

Writer's Checklist

☑ Will the reader know how I feel?

☑ Does my sentence show strong feeling?

☑ Does my exclamation end with an exclamation mark?

Teamwork

Talk About It

How does a team work together?

LOG ON Find out more about teamwork at **www.macmillanmh.com**

Words to Know

help
now
use
very

Ha**nk**
ha**nd**s

Read to Find Out

How will Hank and the girl work together?

Help for Hank

by Linda B. Ross

illustrated by Elivia Savadier

I like to **help** Hank.

I help him dig.

Now I **use** my hands.

It looks **very** good!

Comprehension

Genre
Nonfiction gives information about a topic.

Text Structure
FCAT Author's Purpose
As you read, use your **Author's Purpose Chart.**

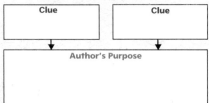

Read to Find Out
Why did the author write *Soccer*?

Soccer

by Patrick Lee

photographs by
Ken Cavanagh

121

We play soccer.

Frank will **help**.
We like Frank.

We run and run.

I run and kick.

I run **very** fast.

I can not **use** my hands.

I kick the ball.
I pass it to Jill.

Now I zig and zag.
I am fast.

I can use my hands.
I am very quick.

Now I grab the ball.

The ball lands in the grass.
It was a very good grab.

Now the game is over.
We like soccer!

Meet the Photographer

Ken Cavanagh says, "Many photographers like to take pictures of one or two things, like sports or family events. I enjoy taking pictures of many things. Besides sports, I like to take pictures of people, places, and nature."

LOG ON Find out more about Ken Cavanagh at **www.macmillanmh.com**

FCAT Photographer's Purpose

Ken Cavanagh wanted to show how soccer is played. Draw someone playing a sport. Label the picture.

FCAT Comprehension Check

Retell the Selection

Use the Retelling Cards to retell the selection in order.

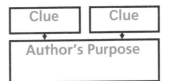

Retelling Cards

Clue	Clue
Author's Purpose	

Think and Compare

1. What did the author want you to learn from the selection?

2. What games do you like to play? Why do you like them?

3. How do soccer players work as a team?

4. How does the soccer team use teamwork like Hank and the girl in "Help for Hank"?

Poetry

Genre
In a **Poem**, words often rhyme.

Literary Element
Words that **Rhyme** end with the same sound.

LOG ON Find out more about teamwork at
www.macmillanmh.com

READ TOGETHER

Guess What!

by Michael R. Strickland

Black and white
Kicked with might

Smooth and round
Air bound

Passed and rolled
Toward the goal

Rise and fall
A soccer ball.

Connect and Compare
What do both *Soccer* and "Guess What!"
tell about how to play soccer?

Writing

Writing Sentences

A **sentence** begins with a capital letter and ends with a special mark.

Write About a Sport

Pat wrote about baseball.

Baseball is the best sport.
I like to hit the ball.

138

Your Turn

Many kids play sports.

Think about a sport you like.

Tell why other kids may like this sport.

Writer's Checklist

☑ Did I tell why I like the sport?

☑ Does each sentence tell a complete thought?

☑ Does each sentence begin with a capital letter?

Jill and Nat

Jill is six.

She digs in the sand.

She plays with Nat.

Nat is six, too.

He rides up the hill.

He rides down the hill.

Cats and Dogs

A cat can jump.
A cat can go up a tree.

A cat can move its ears.
It can move its whiskers.
It can lick its paws.

Look at the cat on the grass.
The cat goes "Purr!"

whiskers

paw

ear

A dog can run.
A dog can jump, too.

A dog has a good nose.
A dog can dig and dig.
It can dig with its paws.

Look at the dog wag its tail.
The dog goes "Woof!"

Glossary

What is a Glossary?

A glossary can help you find the meanings of words. The words are listed in alphabetical order. You can look up a word and read it in a sentence. There is a picture to help you.

Sample Entry

Letter

Main Entry

Sentence

M m

mat

I wipe my feet on the **mat**.

Bb

bat

I hit the ball with my **bat**.

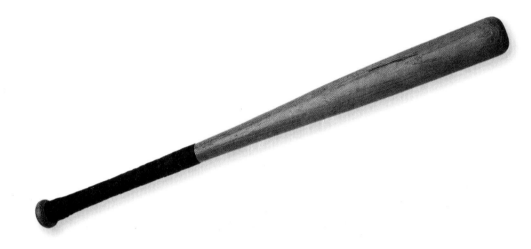

Dd

dig

We can **dig** in the sand.

Ff

fast

I run **fast**.

fly

Birds **fly** in the sky.

Gg

grab

Grab the kitten before it gets away.

Hh

hat

The boy has a red **hat**.

help

Amy gets **help** from her dad.

Mm

mat

I wipe my feet on the **mat**.

Nn

nap

Jill takes a **nap** on the couch.

Pp

pet

I love my **pet** dog.